Mopeds, scooters, and other fuel-efficient automobiles

Mopeds, scooters, and other fuel-efficient automobiles

Chapter 1
Introduction   Page 4

Chapter 2
Types of Fuel Efficient Vehicles   Page 5

Chapter 3
Motorcycles   Page 6

Chapter 4
Mopeds   Page 9

Chapter 5
Scooters   Page 11

Chapter 6
Hybrids   Page 12

Chapter 7
Bio-Diesel Power   Page 17

Chapter 8
Top Gas Powered Cars that are Fuel Efficient   Page 20

Chapter 9
Conclusion   Page 24

Chapter 1
Introduction

The cost of gas is more now than it has every been. In many locations people are paying twice as much per gallon as they were two years ago. There is information circulating in the news and online that the prices are just going to continue to get higher.

This has many consumers very concerned as they don't know what they should do. Certainly they can't afford to continue just paying the posted price at the pumps. Yet they can't stop going to work or about their daily routine that requires them to use a vehicle.

A good strategy that many people are leaning towards more and more is more fuel efficient vehicles. These can get you where you need to go with less gas being used. Of course you want to be able to do so comfortably and safely as well as saving money.

You have several options when it comes to fuel efficient vehicles so take your time to evaluate them and make a good choice. You may find a combination of them is the way to go. For example a motorcycle to get to work and then a fuel efficient hybrid car for the family to get around in.

There are plenty of benefits to each of the various fuel efficiency vehicles as well as some disadvantages. We will go over each of these areas for them so you can make a well informed decision that works for you.

The goal is to be safe, save money, and to be comfortable. You should be able to find at least one fuel efficient vehicle that can do this. Once you are done reading this you should have all the information you need to make a decision that is right for you.

Chapter 2
Types of Fuel Efficient Vehicles

It is important that you understand your options when it comes to fuel efficient vehicles. There are many different types that you can choose from. Some of them only have two wheels while others have four. In the category of two wheels you have motorcycles, mopeds, and scooters.

In many ways they are all the same but there are enough significant differences to classify them differently. For example a motorcycle can obtain much higher speeds that a moped or scooter. There are also laws that pertain to where you can ride mopeds and scooters.

They often aren't allowed on highways and freeways were there is a very high speed limit. They are mainly used for in town riding. There is also a lower age limit in many areas for them than motorcycles. You will have to refer to the specific laws and regulations in your particular area though.

Those fuel efficient vehicles that feature four wheels include hybrids, those that operate off of bio-diesel, and fuel efficient gas powered cars. All of them feature a variety of different models by various manufacturers. Since they are becoming more in demand you will find that more of them are being offered in order to keep up with consumer demands.

Chapter 3

Motorcycles

In the past it seems that motorcycles were only used by most people as a secondary vehicle. They allowed a person to get out into the open environment and enjoy a nice day. They were also great for long road trips when you wanted to see what the open road had to offer you. Today you will notice many more motorcycles out there on the road due to the cost of fuel. People are using them to commute to work and to complete other essential travels. You can get many more miles out of a motorcycle than a car.

Yet you can't rely upon a motorcycle when they weather is bad. If you live in a region where the temperatures turn really cold and snow is common then that motorcycle will need to be stored. You may be on it and end up in a rain storm on a sunny afternoon as well.

You also can't drive a motorcycle to the grocery store or to pick up the dry cleaning. Even so, you can use it as much as possible when the weather is nice and you don't have such errands to run. That will save you money on gas a great deal of the time anyway.

Then you can use your other vehicle for the rest of the time and do your best to cut costs on it any way that you can when it comes to filling up at the pump. Just make sure you take a look at the cost of motorcycle insurance and other factors so you can budget for the cost.

Since you are out in the open there is more risk of serious injury when you get involved in a motorcycle accident. Too many motorists on the road don't pay attention to motorcycles as they are small. They can end up in the blind spot when a driver is attempting to switch lanes as well.

Make sure you always wear long pants, a long sleeved shirt, and a helmet when you operate a motorcycle. You want to protect your body as much as you can in the event that any accident does occur. A helmet can definitely save your life so don't leave it behind even if you are only going for a very short trip.

Motorcycle prices are relatively affordable though but it depends on what you want. The size of the motor as well as the brand will influence the price. You can get a stock model or have one custom make for you. Make sure you compare the cost of a new one versus a used one so you can get the best deal.

Of course not everyone is comfortable operating a motorcycle. It can take time to learn the rules of it. You don't want to buy one until you know how to operate one. See if you can get a friend or family member to help you learn on their motorcycle.

Some retailers will offer free lessons too if they know you are interested in learning to ride. Ask about this to see what details they can provide. Take your time to get comfortable on a motorcycle though before you rush into driving it on the road with other vehicles.

It isn't just men who are out there looking at motorcycles though. Many women are as well. In fact, there are certain models of them offered by top manufacturers including Harley Davidson just for women. They are lighter so they won't be as difficult to keep balanced.

Take the time to make sure any motorcycle you are going to operate is a good match for your size. You should be able to touch the ground with both feed flat when you have it level. The weight of it needs to be manageable for you as well.

Be sure to check the distance between your arms and the handle bars. If you aren't comfortable then you need one with a shorter reach. There are different sizes of engines in motorcycles and that will result in various amounts of power behind the throttle. Make sure you take a look at what is offered so you won't have any surprises.

You may need to take a written and verbal test at your local DMV in order to obtain a motorcycle license as well. Check to see what regulations are in place in your area. That way you aren't breaking the law in any way in order to save money on gas prices.

Chapter 4
Mopeds

A moped is similar to a motorcycle in a variety of ways. It isn't a mode of fuel efficient transportation that you can use to travel on the highways though. The highest speed they offer is about 31 miles per hour. You would be a hazard to yourself and others on busy roads only going that fast.

A moped features a very small engine as well. They don't offer anything more than a 50cc motor. This means you will have enough power to get out there and do what you need to but not enough to really harm yourself. Still, you should always wear a helmet when you operate one just to be safe.

In most states you must be at least 16 years of age to get a valid license to operate one. This often requires completing a course of instruction as well as a written test. The rules can vary so make sure you find out how they apply in your own area.

For example in many locations if you already have a valid driver's license in that state that was issued before 2001 you are exempt from the above process. You are automatically able to operate a moped in town without having to obtain the additional licensing.

They are really great for in town though and they are very simple to operate. It doesn't take as much effort to balance one as it does with a motorcycle. That is because they are extremely lightweight. They also cost only a couple of thousand dollars new. You can get a used one for even less than that if you take the time to look in the right places.

Most of the mopeds out there feature a basket on the front so you can place some items in there. So if you drive it to town to run errands you can have a place to put the few things you are picking up. You won't be able to do a large amount of shopping but you will have enough room for a few basic items.

Chapter 5
Scooters

Scooters are a notch below mopeds in terms of speed. They aren't going to go more than 20 miles per hour with the electric models. Still, you can use them to get around faster and easier than using a regular bicycle. The are great if you live in a small area where things are relatively close. You may not have public transportation available so this can help.

The laws are very different when it comes to who can legally operate a scooter. it also depends on the type. In some areas children as young as 12 years of age are able to do so. In other places though you must be the same age as required to legally operate a vehicle and have a valid driver's license.

There are small sized scooters where you stand on a board that is similar to a skateboard. Some models have an extremely thin board to stand on. There is a handle that should be adjustable to your height that you use to maneuver the scooter. It is shaped like the letter T.

There will be a small gas tank on the side of it that holds up to five gallons of gas depending on the type of scooter that you have. Many of them have a pull start mechanism that you need to engage before you can get the fuel to run through the system and give you the necessary power to move about.

Some of the more expensive scooters look like mopeds but they operate with the use of a battery and electricity. These models may or may not use gas depending on which model you select. Those that do require the use of gas aren't going to consume very much of it though at any given time.

Chapter 6
Hybrids

Not everyone is comfortable with a fuel efficiency vehicle that only has two wheels though. There shouldn't be a push for a person who isn't confident in their ability to operate one to have to do so. This can result in a accident occurring and that isn't worth saving money on fuel costs.

For other people, those types of vehicles just aren't practical. You may have a family so you need to drop the baby at daycare and another child off at school. You can't do that without a regular vehicle.

You may live in an area where it is too cold for most of the year to get any real use out of those two wheeled options even though they are fuel efficient. There is no need to worry though as you do have some really good options.

One of them you have likely hear a great deal about is the hybrid. This is a type of vehicle that operates using two different fuel sources. One of them is gasoline and the other is either solar power or electricity. With the solar power, there are cells that charge during the day. With the electricity there are batteries that have to be recharged on a regular basis.

Regardless of which one you choose, gasoline will be the back up fuel source. This means when you don't have any more solar power in the cells or any more electricity in the batteries you will switch over to the gasoline that is in your vehicle.

Once you have the opportunity to recharge the main energy source, it will switch back over. You don't have to do anything to get the vehicle to go from one power source to the next. It will be an automatic switch over and it can happen in the middle of your commute to work. You won't lose power in the vehicle so don't worry about the speed limit that you are driving.

A hybrid vehicle is designed to be able to save energy in ways that ordinary vehicles can't. Pushing on the brakes of your vehicle is a common practice. It helps you to slow down when you need to as well as to completely stop your vehicle.

In a regular vehicle the braking process results in more fuel being used. This is because they car has to get back to a certain speed and it takes fuel to do so. Hybrids rely on a process known as regenerative braking. Instead of using more fuel you will actually create more energy each time you step on the brakes.

All hybrids also have an automatic shut off sensor. This means when you roll up to a stop sign the engine will completely stop. As soon as you step on the gas pedal though it will restart. As a result the excess idling that adds up and wastes fuel is completely eliminated.

A smaller motor is used in hybrid vehicles so it takes less fuel to give them the necessary power. However, you don't have to worry about not having enough power to go the proper speed limit or anything like that.

Some people have a fear that a hybrid will be slow and that it will just leave them stranded due to not enough energy. This isn't a scenario that will ever become a reality for anyone with a hybrid vehicle.

They are very well made and for years they were researched before offered to the general public. In fact, hybrids were tested by companies all over the world including the various branches of the United States military.

For those individuals who want to continue driving larger sized vehicles, a hybrid can be the perfect solution. There are small vehicles but also the large ones including the Yukon by GMC and the Tahoe by Chevrolet. Both of these were added in 2008 to meet consumer demands.

These hybrid vehicles are expensive though and that is what often prevents consumers from buying them. The would love to own one in order to save money and to protect the environment. However, financially they may not be able to meet the monthly obligation of getting such a fuel efficient vehicle.

The government does offer some very nice incentives though. When you file your income tax return you can claim a huge deduction for the year in which you purchase your hybrid. This can be something to really entice those who are sitting on the fence to move forward with their purchase.

You will find though that for many types of hybrid vehicles there is a waiting list. That is because the manufacturers have limited the number of them that they make. Of course they have been looking at increasing those numbers due to the number of consumers after them these days.

High gas prices at the pump that don't look like they will be dropping any time soon are encouraging more consumers in the market for a new vehicle to look at them. They want to do all they can to get a reliable vehicle, protect the environment, and cut down on the amount of money they pay for fuel.

However, there have been reports that there is a shortage of the necessary materials required to make a quality hybrid vehicle. A key element that must be used to make the electric motors for hybrids as well as the propulsion system for the batteries require the use of Dysprosium.

This particular element is rare and most of it is found in China. Yet they aren't willing to share too much of it because they rely upon the use of Dysprosium for their electronic gadgets that they sale all over the world. In the mean time researchers to continue to look for alternative elements that may be able to work in place of the Dysprosium.

Some people have the image of a hybrid vehicle being strange looking but that couldn't be further from the truth. There are many common models of vehicle son the road that are this design. You may drive with them on the same roads each day and just not realize it.

There are many terrific hybrid vehicles you can choose from out there. You should take a look online for a complete list of them but here is some information on some of the common ones. You can anticipate spending from $27,000 to $64,000 on one depending on the model you are most interested in.

One of the top selling hybrids is the Honda Civic. Not only is it a top compact car for comfort and style, the original models are very fuel efficient as well. This means when you do need to switch over from electricity or solar power to fuel you won't be consuming very much of it in the process.

With the rate of 45 miles to the gallon as a hybrid on the highway and 40 in town you certainly should be checking into this type of hybrid. It is relatively high priced though which is the down side of things. However, it can certainly prove to be quite a good investment that will save you plenty of money in fuel to compensate for that.

The Nissan Altima is one of the most affordable hybrid cars out there. It also features a simple yet sophisticated design so people really like it. This is a classy car without going to the extremes. It does very well with fuel efficiency as well.

On the highway you can expect to get 42 miles per gallon. In town you should still get about 35.

The most expensive hybrid vehicle that you will come across is the Mercedes Benz. This is a very sophisticated model that comes with a hefty price tag as well. It offers all the features of a sports car though including fast speeds. It has the luxury too with very comfortable seats and all the options you can imagine.

There are many models of hybrid vehicles that will be emerging on the market for 2009. Most of them will be out in October or November of 2008. They include the Audi Q7, Cadillac Escalade, Chevrolet Silverado pickup, Dodge Durango, GMC Sierra pickup, Saturn Vue, Toyota Sienna which will be a hybrid minivan, and the Toyota Prius.

As you can see there are many new options that will soon be available for consumers in the way of hybrid vehicles. This is very exciting to those tired of paying very high prices. You can get a sneak peek at the 2009 hybrid models at various car shows around the United States. Go online to find out when one will be in your area.

If you find one you really like, it may be a good idea to deal with the manufacturer directly. They can help you to reserve one now so you won't be on a waiting list later on. You can even have it customized with the accessories you want, the interior you choose, and the exterior color that you will be very happy with.

Chapter 7
Bio-Diesel Power

An option many consumers are interested in is bio-diesel power. This is a type of alternative power that means you won't be relying upon gasoline in order to power your vehicle. It may sound crazy but this process involves using vegetable oil to keep your vehicle running.

The problem though is that the use of bio-diesel isn't standard in the United States. So getting you hands on what you need at times can prove to be difficult. Yet many consumers say they don't have any problems with their vehicles using this type of alternative fuel. It keeps the insides of it well lubricated and the oil stays clean.

There are starting to be more places though where you can get bio-diesel fuel at the pumps though. This is exciting for those who manufacture such vehicles as well as those consumers interested in buying them. It is sold for a price that is significantly lower than standard fuel as well.

Other consumers with bio-diesel vehicles are content to place fresh vegetable oil into their vehicles. Some people have been known to also use the used vegetable oil from restaurants without experiencing any problems. This is a very creative way to stop being robbed blind at the gas station.

Of course that used vegetable oil can't be dumped directly into your vehicle in such a condition. Instead it has to be processed to remove pieces of food, various debris, and glycerin found in such forms of used vegetable oil. Failure to remove them will prevent your vehicle from operating like it should.

The fact that the use of bio-diesel fuel also results in less emissions into the air is important as well. Not only will you save money on fuel but you will be doing your part to protect the environment as well. Many people are buying conversion kits so they can start using bio-diesel and stop buying gasoline. This type of conversion can only be completed accurately if you have a diesel vehicle.

You can also choose to buy a bio-diesel vehicle directly from various dealers. Some of the top vehicle manufacturers now offer such models for customers to choose from. All of the Volkswagen models can be purchased with the bio-diesel option.

Large sized pickups are often ran by diesel fuel. You will find most of them offered by various manufacturers including Chevy, Ford, and Dodge all offer them. Some foreign options include Volvo and Mercedes. Right now Jeep has a new model that is getting ready for production to take off.

A person with these types of vehicles often needs a great deal of power behind them to get the job accomplished. It is important to realize that there is no difference between a regular heavy duty vehicle that operates on diesel fuel and one that operates on bio-diesel fuel except for that source of energy.

The power of the vehicle will remain the same regardless of which one you use. One issue that has become quite a concern though is that bio-diesel vehicles can be very tough to start in colder weather. This is due to the fact that the materials used to make it become thick during that time of the year.

A solution to this that has been working well is to mix the bio-diesel fuel with some petroleum. Generally this is a mix of 80% bio-diesel and 20% petroleum to get a good balance. The amount of petroleum that will be added though depends on how cold of a climate you live in.

Since bio-diesel is man made we will always have enough of it. There is a limit to the natural resources we have. Once they are depleted we will never be able to use them again. Saving what we do have for future generations is something to consider.

It can be very expensive to buy a bio-diesel vehicle though and that is what often holds many consumers back from doing so. Add that to the fact that they are skeptical about vegetable being suitable for a vehicle to operate on. As a society we get too comfortable with the norm and that can hinder advancement for us in many aspects.

Chapter 8
Top Gas Powered Cars that are Fuel Efficient

You may find it is time to either trade in your gas guzzler or to purchase an additional vehicle that is fuel efficient. There are some really great ones out there offered by the best manufactures. Many of the best are compact cars but some of them are medium in size.

You may have the image of being squeezed into a seat that is too small and not enough room for your groceries. Yet most of these fuel efficient cars are roomier than you might think. It can be helpful to take your entire family to look for one. This way you can see just how good of a fit it would end up being.

This is a smart move as you may have a child or two that use car seats. They do take up more room but you want to find out for sure how everyone is going to fit. Saving money on gas isn't going to be something you care about too much if everyone in the car is complaining about not enough space each time they get into it.

The Ford Focus gets the top billing when it comes to fuel efficient cars. This is also a very affordable car to buy either new or used. They come with two or four doors so you can decide which model is best for you. It should get you between 28-30 miles per gallon on the highway and 24 in town.

The Honda Fit is similar with a hatch back as well as two or four doors. It does get better gas mileage though at a rate of 34 miles per gallon on the highway and 28 in town. It isn't as comfortable overall as the Ford Focus though so that is why it doesn't get top billing.

Honda also comes in at #3 with the Civic. This is a car they have had around for quite some time. It has always been very fuel efficient but more people are interested in it now than before due to the high fuel prices. It offers up to 36 miles per gallon on the highway and 25 in town.

The most expensive fuel efficient vehicle out there is the Mercedes Benz. These are very stylish vehicles and often driven by those who want to let their prestige shine. This is an extremely well built vehicle that is also extremely fast. Most people only dream of owning such a fabulous car though as they are out of the price range for most of us. They do offer 32 miles per gallon on the highway about 25 in town.

Completing the top five is the mini Cooper. This is likely the most fun you will have with a fuel efficient car. They offer plenty of room inside and a great style with the exterior. They are more common with women than with men though as they tend to be labeled as cute.

If you weren't impressed with the power it offered in the past, you should look at the newer models. BMW has been listening to consumers and the Mini Cooper now features more power than ever before. In addition to being fuel efficient it is also very environmentally friendly.

When you see that it gets 37 miles to the gallon on the highway and 28 in town you will definitely be impressed! They have a decent price too so you won't find it to be too unreasonable to fit into your budget. The money you save on gas for it can go towards paying your payment on it each month!

Spots 6 and 7 in the top 10 fuel efficient vehicles are both by Nissan. First you have the Nissan Altima which is a medium sized vehicle. It has a nice rounded design along the back side which makes it look more expensive than it really is.

The fuel savings won't be as high as with some of the other vehicles we have talked about.

Yet if comfort is very important to you then this could be the one to choose. You will be able to get 31 miles per gallon on the highway and 32 in town. This is a 4-cylinder vehicle that has enough power to keep even a picky car owner very satisfied.

Next is the Nissan Sentra which offers just about the same miles per gallon as the sister Altima does. The main difference is that his sedan is an automatic while just about all of the other fuel efficiency vehicles including the Altima are manual.

Watch out for bigger and better things on the horizon from Toyota in the area of fuel efficient vehicles as well. They are very proud to be filling up the last three slots on the top ten countdown. The fact that they have more vehicles on this list than any other manufacturer means they really are dedicated to helping both the environment and consumers.

The Toyota Camry has always been well loved by consumers as it is a well designed vehicle. It is comfortable and it handles extremely well. This was one of the top selling models for years before gas prices became so difficult to fit into the budget.

This particular vehicle is also available as a hybrid but there is a long waiting list to get your hands on one right now. The regular model offers about the same miles per gallon both on the highway and in town with a number of about 34. However, the hybrid will give you about 44 miles per gallon which is significantly higher.

The Toyota Corolla is a smaller model than the Camry but still a very good vehicle. It is less expensive as well so if you are looking to get something to work well in your budget this could be it. If you haven't been impressed with the body style though keep an eye out for the new design in 2009.

The Toyota Corolla is available in both manual and automatic transmissions which is nice for consumers. Which one you choose won't make too much of a difference as far as your fuel mileage is concerned though. You should be able to get 35 miles per gallon on the highway and 26 miles per gallon in town.

You will be amazed at the gas savings you will get with the number ten on the list. It is the Toyota Prius which can get 48 miles per gallon on the highway and 45 on the highway. Many consumers don't like the style of this vehicle though. They feel the back end looks smashed or like it wasn't finished. The square look can make the entire vehicle look odd.

Yet if you really want something that is going to save you money at the pump, this fuel efficient vehicle can certainly do so. It does have a futuristic look to it that many people just aren't ready for yet. While they agree it handles nice and is roomy, it can be hard to commit to a vehicle you aren't going to want to see in your driveway each morning.

Chapter 9
Conclusion

With the cost of a gallon gas around $4 as the National average, it is understood that many consumers are very upset about what it costs to put enough fuel in their vehicle to get around. Depending on the type of vehicle you have your overall cost will vary. It also depends on how many miles you put on your vehicle in a given span of time.

As a result of these continuous increases, consumers are left feeling helpless. Many of them are turning to fuel efficient vehicles that offer them the chance to pay less for fuel though. They may be trading on their current vehicle for something else or buying an additional vehicle to help them cut costs.

This may be in the form of a new vehicle or a used one that still have plenty of life left in it. Being able to calculate the differences between the ongoing cost of fuel for you right now and what you will be paying if you do get a different vehicle is important.

That way you can determine if the purchase will be cost effective in the long run for you or not. There is no point of doing it though if you aren't able to get a great return on your investment. The information you just read should help you to determine which type of fuel efficient vehicle is right for you.

It may be a two wheeled model such as a motorcycle, moped, or scooter. It really depends on where you will be traveling due to the various speeds that they offer. In addition to being able to save money on fuel with these options though you need to pay attention to some other factors.

For example you need to find out about the licensing requirements in your area. You also need to make safety a priority. Never operate such vehicles when the road conditions aren't right for it. You also need to make it a habit of wearing a helmet. It doesn't matter how fast you will be traveling or how far of a distance.

You can also go with regular vehicles that are more fuel efficient than what you operate right now. This can be in the form of a hybrid, a bio-diesel vehicle, or a fuel efficient model that is offered. All of them can be a great solution when you want some armor around you to protect you when you are on the road. It also provides you with room for more than one passenger.

Hybrid vehicles are more expensive than regular fuel efficient models. This is due to the high demand for them as well as for the cost of making them. They are excellent for the environment though which is refreshing to hear. They also only use fuel when the electricity or solar power that is mainly used is depleted.

The amount of gas you will use depends on how long it is before you are able to restore that main power source to the hybrid. Even when you are relying upon the gas though for power you will get an amazing amount of miles per gallon of fuel.

Bio-diesel is a type of alternative fuel that can be used instead of gasoline to operate your vehicle. You can modify older vehicles that have a diesel system in them with a converter kit. This can cost a couple of thousand dollars but can prove to be very cost effective.

There are also bio-diesel vehicles you can buy new from the manufacturer. They operate with the use of vegetable oil and they seem to be vehicles that will last a very long time. They also don't release as many emissions into the environment as other vehicles on our roads do.

The list of the top ten fuel efficient vehicles on the market right now should prove to be very helpful. If you are in the market for a new vehicle then take a look at them to see what you like. Should you decide to go with another model of vehicle you should look up the information on it before you buy it.

While you may love the look of a particular vehicle, the fact is that you may end up struggling continually to pay for the gas that you must put inside of it. That isn't going to benefit you in any way so make sure the amount of miles per gallon you can expect from what you buy is going to be something you can work with.

Remember that fuel prices are expected to continue rising. That cost is something you need to think about when you shop for a fuel efficient vehicle. It also needs to be safe and to offer you enough room. Even though you want to maximize fuel savings you need to be realistic.

It won't work well to cram your family of five into a Ford Focus even though it offers really great fuel mileage. You will need to go with a medium sized fuel efficient vehicle that may not get as good of gas mileage but you will all fit into it comfortably.

This type of trade off is important to keep you all happy. You certainly don't want to ride to work each day in a vehicle that has your knees pressed tightly up against the dashboard. Paying attention to such details is important with the majority of fuel efficient vehicles being compact cars.

If a larger vehicle is what you need then do your best to find one that is decent in regards to the fuel mileage it gets. Before fuel is up to $5 a gallon which is predicted by the end of the summer you need to have a plan of action. You can sit around and let the cost continue to stress you out or you can use a method of transportation that is more fuel efficient.

Hopefully you will be able to soon implement one of these fuel saving vehicles into your lifestyle. You will be able to breath easier when you drive to the gas station and see the prices posted for fuel. There is quite a demand for these vehicles these days so the sooner you start to look the better deal you can secure.

www.ingramcontent.com/pod-product-compliance
Lightning Source LLC
LaVergne TN
LVHW021055100526
838202LV00083B/6237